SELF-LOVE:

Affirmations Activity Book for Black Girls

Book 2 of the Self-Love Journey Series for Black Girls

This Book Belongs to:

i'm UNIQUE

SUPPORT OUR MOVEMENT!

SCAN ME

Thanks for the support!

Scan the QR Code to follow us, explore our other books, and share your review.

The Perfect Daily Companion Journal, Book 1 of the Self-Love Journey series.

SELF-LOVE JOURNEY
A Daily Journal for Black Girls

LET'S MAKE TODAY A HAPPY DAY

I AM ENOUGH!

Black & beautiful

DREAM BIG

Live the Life You've Always Wanted. Step-by-step guide for adults.

THE MILLENNIAL RESET

A SELF-HELP GUIDE TO STOP OVERTHINKING & OVERCOME SELF-DOUBT

UNSURE · DEPRESSION · LOST · OVERTHINKING · STRESS · ANXIETY · CONFUSED · TRAUMA · WORRY · SELF-DOUBT · PANIC · INSECURE · FEAR · STUCK

COGNITIVE BEHAVIORAL AND DIALECTICAL BEHAVIORAL APPROACH FOR ADULTS

K. QUEN PENN
EMPOWERUS BOOKS & PUBLISHING

Activity Book Instructions:

Parents - This book is a 52-week, weekly affirmations activity book:

1. *Read Affirmation:* Recite the affirmation for the week each day.
2. *Journal Prompt:* Write a few sentences to answer the daily journal prompts.
3. *Drawing:* Create drawings that illustrate your responses to the prompts.
4. *Coloring:* Decorate and color the pages to show your creativity.

Each weekly affirmation is designed to be used once a week and recited daily during that week.

The monthly affirmation is meant to be said consistently throughout the entire month.

Purpose: Reciting affirmations helps children feel comfortable speaking positively about themselves and fosters a habit of affirming self-worth.

Follow this example below:

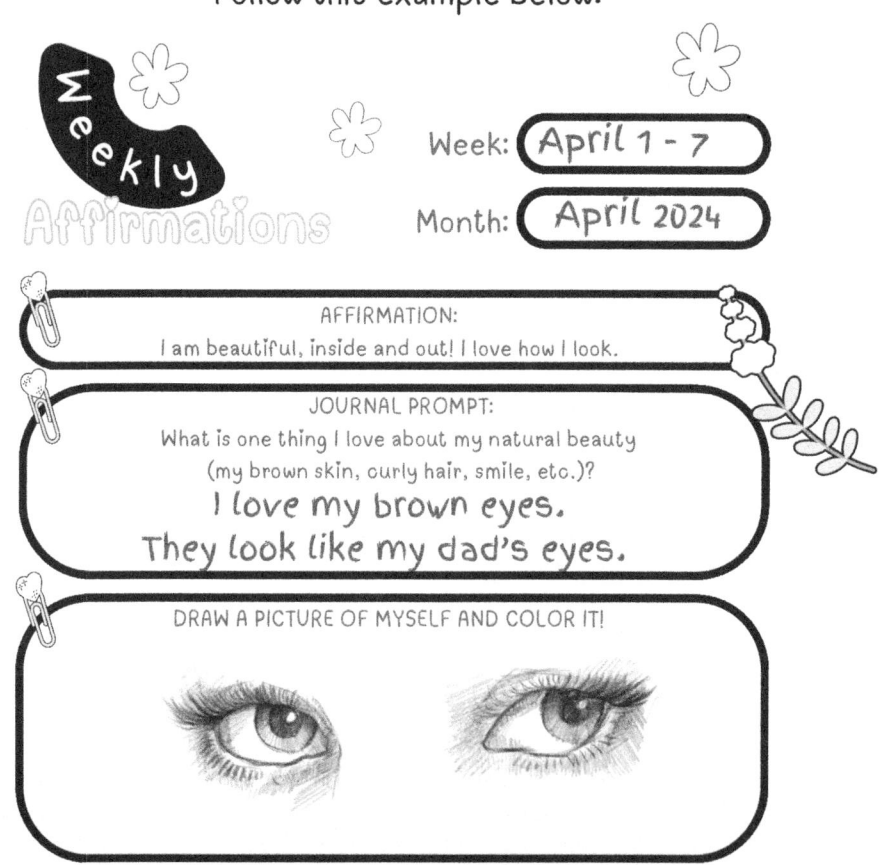

Weekly Affirmations

Week: April 1 - 7

Month: April 2024

AFFIRMATION:
I am beautiful, inside and out! I love how I look.

JOURNAL PROMPT:
What is one thing I love about my natural beauty (my brown skin, curly hair, smile, etc.)?
I love my brown eyes.
They look like my dad's eyes.

DRAW A PICTURE OF MYSELF AND COLOR IT!

Positive Morning Routine
CHECKLIST

- Wake up

- Make bed and pray

- Positive Affirmations:
  I am... I can... I will...

- Drink a glass of water

- Bathe and brush teeth

- Style my curls and baby hairs

- A cute outfit and accessories

- Eat a healthy breakfast

- Pack backpack and lunch

- Start my day with a smile

Weekly Affirmations

Week:

Month:

AFFIRMATION:
I am beautiful, inside and out! I love how I look.

JOURNAL PROMPT:
What is one thing I love about my natural beauty (my brown skin, curly hair, smile, etc.)?

DRAW A PICTURE OF YOURSELF AND COLOR IT!

Weekly Affirmations

Week:

Month:

AFFIRMATION:
My skin is a perfectly melanated brown! It shines like the sun!

JOURNAL PROMPT:
What are some things that make me proud of my skin color.

Weekly Affirmations

Week:

Month:

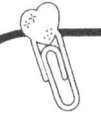

AFFIRMATION:
I am a young Black queen! I am strong like my ancestors.

JOURNAL PROMPT:
When have I felt strong?
How did my strength help me face a challenge?

Weekly Affirmations

Week:

Month:

AFFIRMATION:
I am proud of my Black heritage and everything that makes me who I am!

JOURNAL PROMPT:
What makes me proud of my culture?
Is it our style, food, music, rhythm, or a piece of Black history?

January Affirmations

My black is beautiful.

My melanin is a perfect shade of beige, brown, and gold.

My curly hair and baby hairs are magical.

My black features are gorgeous and connect me to my roots.

I celebrate my unique beauty.

I am enough

I am CAPABLE

Weekly Affirmations

Week:

Month:

AFFIRMATION:
My voice matters! I have some important and valuable things to say.

JOURNAL PROMPT:
When have I spoken up for myself or others?
How did it make me feel?

Weekly Affirmations

Week:

Month:

AFFIRMATION:
I am confident! I trust in my abilities!

JOURNAL PROMPT:
What is one thing I do well?
How can I use this skill to help others?

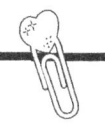

DRAW A PICTURE OF YOUR TALENTS AND COLOR IT!

Weekly Affirmations

Week:

Month:

AFFIRMATION:
My natural hair is magical! I can style it in many cute ways like a fluffy afro, cute puffs, or even braids, dreads, and twists with bright beads.

JOURNAL PROMPT:
What is my favorite hairstyle that makes my beautiful hair shine, and why does it make me feel so good?

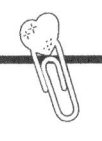

DRAW YOUR FAVORITE HAIRSTYLE AND COLOR IT!

Weekly Affirmations

Week:

Month:

AFFIRMATION:
I deserve love, respect, and kindness.

JOURNAL PROMPT:
When do I feel love and respect?
How do I show myself love and respect?

February Affirmations

My Black culture is rich.

We are trendsetters and inventors.

We are more than our history, we make history.

We are Hip Hop, R&B, Soul, Jazz, Rock n Roll, Country, and everything in between.

We had a dream and we are still dreaming.

I am worthy of happiness

NICE

Weekly Affirmations

Week:

Month:

AFFIRMATION:
I am enough just as I am!

JOURNAL PROMPT:
Write about a time when I felt proud of being me.

Weekly Affirmations

Week:

Month:

AFFIRMATION:
I treat my body and mind with care and respect!

JOURNAL PROMPT:
What are some ways I take care of myself?
(exercise, eating healthy, resting, writing in my journal, etc.)

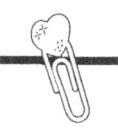

DRAW A PICTURE OF YOUR FAVORITE WAY TO TAKE CARE OF YOURSELF & COLOR IT!

Weekly Affirmations

Week:

Month:

AFFIRMATION:
I take pride in my culture and the beauty it contributes to the world.

JOURNAL PROMPT:
What are some things I am most proud of about my culture, and why?
(Black history, music, dance, style, etc.)

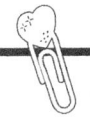

DRAW A PICTURE OF SOME OF YOUR FAVORITE THINGS ABOUT BLACK CULTURE AND COLOR IT!

Weekly Affirmations

Week:

Month:

AFFIRMATION:
I am strong and brave. I can handle any challenge I face.

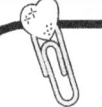

JOURNAL PROMPT:
Think about a hard time. Name some ways I stayed strong.

DRAW A PICTURE OF A PERSON OR THING THAT KEEPS YOU STRONG AND COLOR IT!

March Affirmations

I am smart and capable.

I am a kind and good person.

Each emotion I feel is important.

I treat eveyone with respect.

My mind is creative.

CELEBRATE EVERY WIN, NO MATTER HOW SMALL

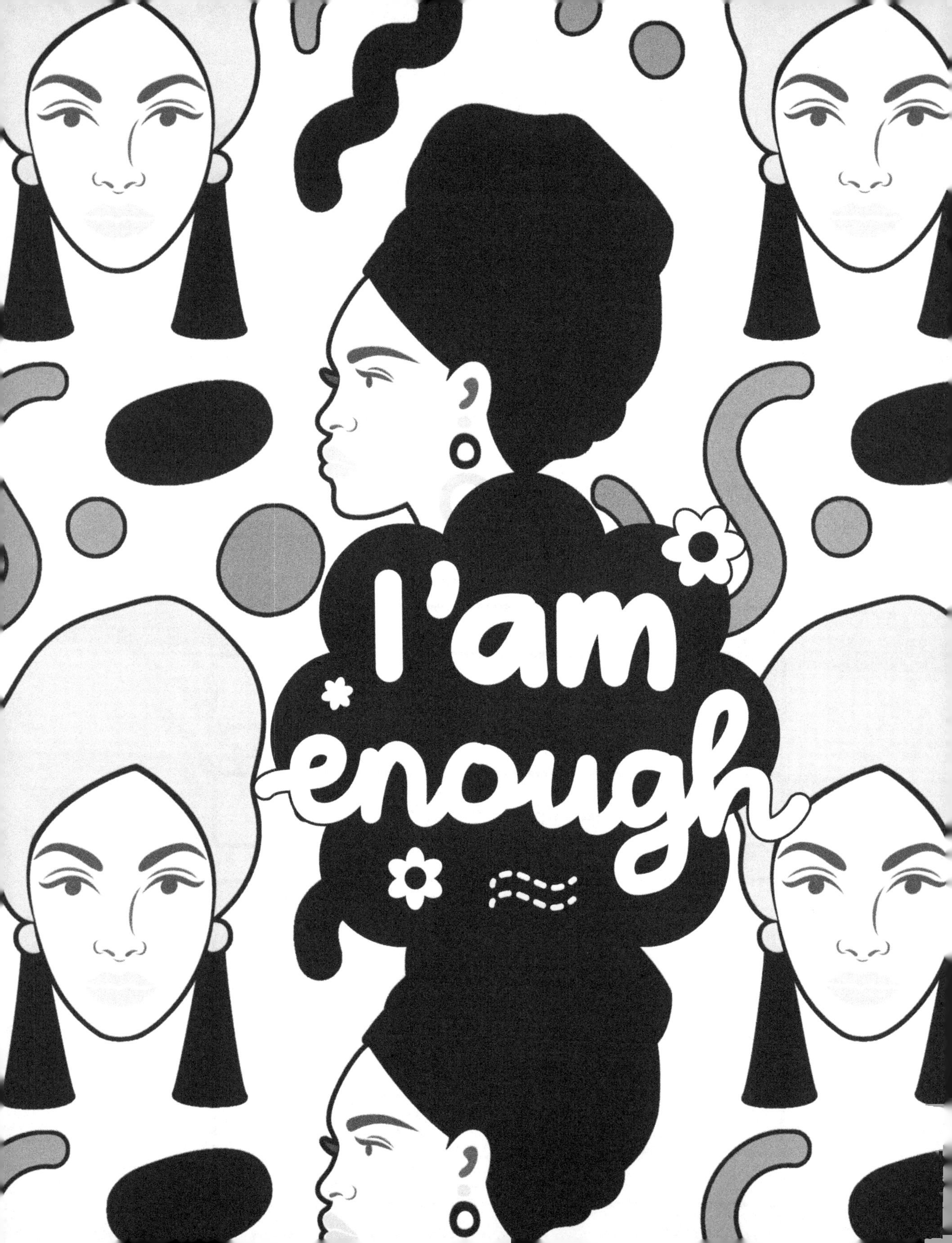
I'am
enough

Weekly Affirmations

Week:

Month:

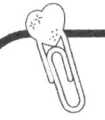

AFFIRMATION:
I celebrate my uniqueness. There is no one else like me!

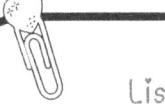

JOURNAL PROMPT:
List some unique things about me that I love and celebrate.

Weekly Affirmations

Week:

Month:

AFFIRMATION:
I choose to see beauty around me.

JOURNAL PROMPT:
Look around. List some things that I see that are beautiful.

DRAW A PICTURE OF SOMETHING BEAUTIFUL THAT YOU SEE AND COLOR IT!

Weekly Affirmations

Week:

Month:

AFFIRMATION:
I am confident. I am proud of my talents and gifts.

JOURNAL PROMPT:
What are some talents or skills that make me special?

DRAW A PICTURE OF TALENT OR SKILL THAT YOU HAVE AND COLOR IT!

Weekly Affirmations

Week:

Month:

AFFIRMATION:
My dreams can come true. I will achieve them!

JOURNAL PROMPT:
Write about one of my dreams or goals.
What steps can I take today to move closer to it?

April Affirmations

I celebrate my uniqueness.

My experiences are special and powerful.

I am heard, seen, and validated.

I can learn valuable lessons from my hard days.

My good days are blessings.

You are LOVED

I embrace my imperfections

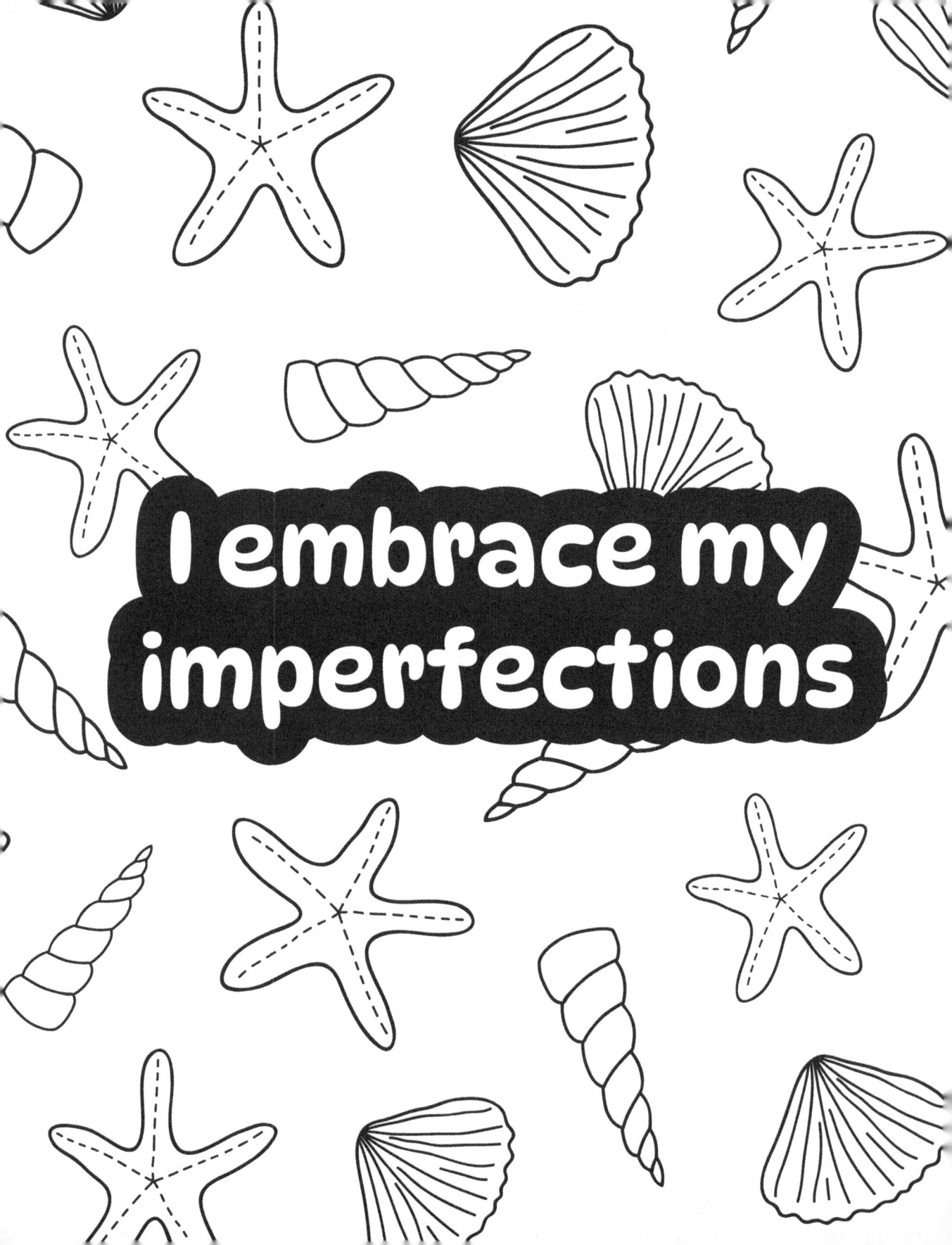

Weekly Affirmations

Week:

Month:

AFFIRMATION:
I believe in myself. I can accomplish anything I set my mind to

JOURNAL PROMPT:
Write about a recent achievement.
How did I feel when I achieved it?

Weekly Affirmations

Week:

Month:

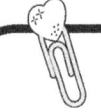

AFFIRMATION:
I am proud of my Black roots! My Black history has shaped me.

JOURNAL PROMPT:
Who is a person from Black history who inspires me?
What made their story so powerful?

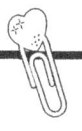

DRAW A PICTURE OF WHY THIS PERSON IS IMPORTANT AND COLOR IT!

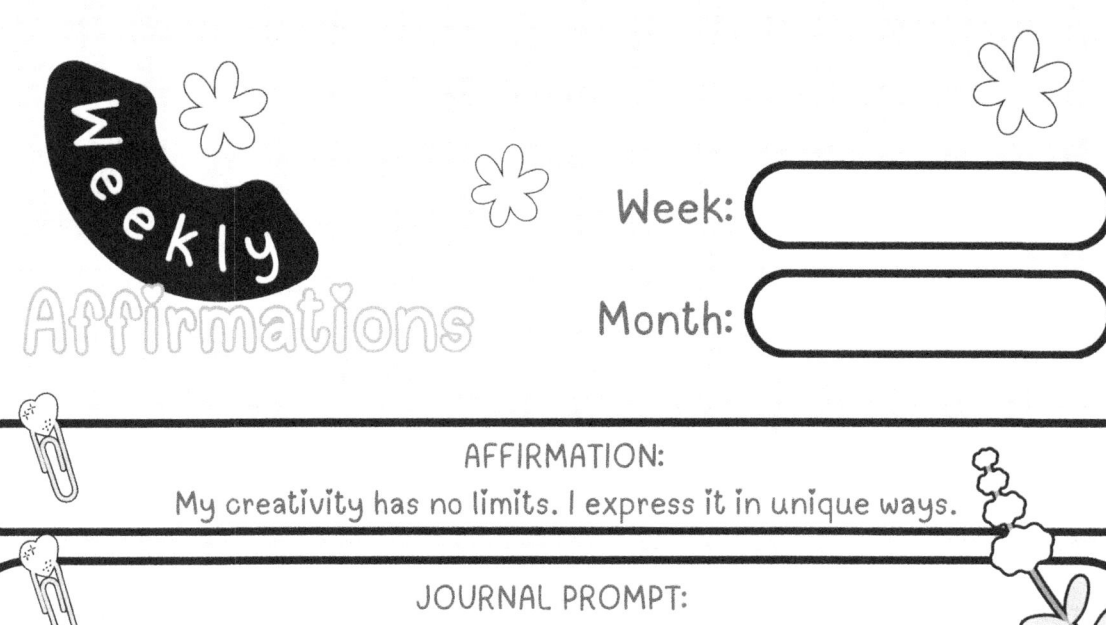

Weekly Affirmations

Week:

Month:

AFFIRMATION:
My creativity has no limits. I express it in unique ways.

JOURNAL PROMPT:
What are some activities I like to do to show my creativity?
How do I feel about myself when I do them?
(Coloring, painting, singing, dancing, etc.)

DRAW A PICTURE OF YOURSELF DOING SOMETHING CREATIVE AND COLOR IT!

Weekly Affirmations

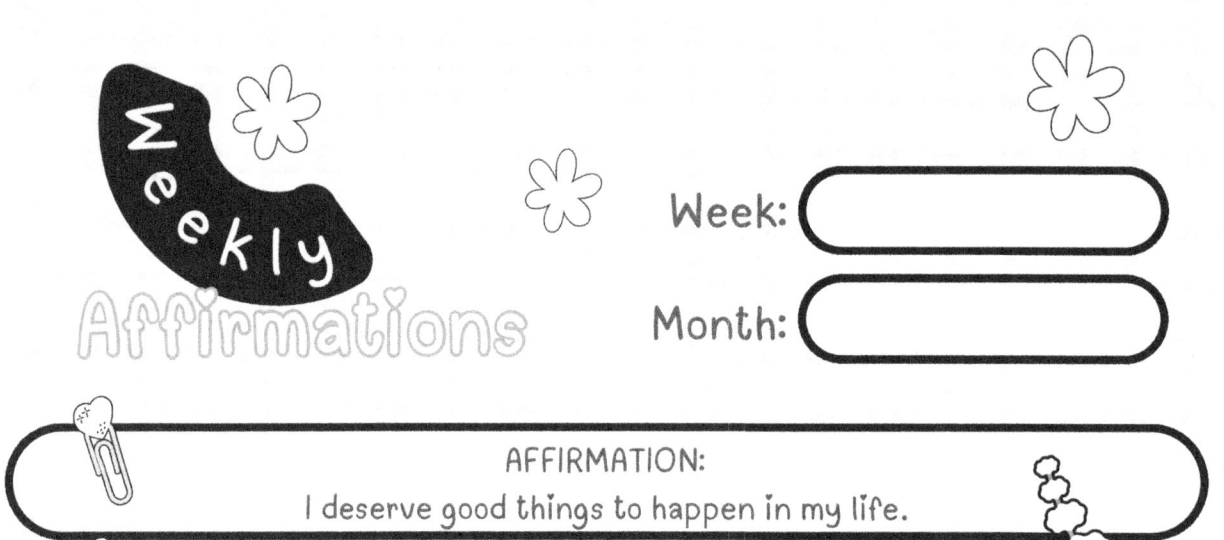

Week:

Month:

AFFIRMATION:
I deserve good things to happen in my life.

JOURNAL PROMPT:
Think about the good things in your life (family, friends, school, etc.). How do I show thankfulness to them?

May Affirmations

I love and I am thankful for my family.

I love and I am thankful for my friends.

I am confident in my appearance.

I am confident in my identity.

I am confident in my abilities.

PRACTICE MAKES progress

it's gonna be okay!

Weekly Affirmations

Week:

Month:

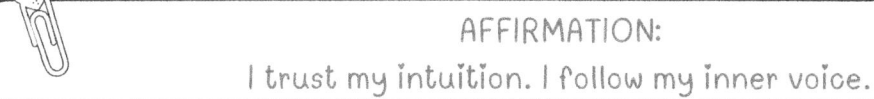

AFFIRMATION:
I trust my intuition. I follow my inner voice.

JOURNAL PROMPT:
Write about a time when I trusted my instincts.
How did I know that I was making the right choice?

Weekly Affirmations

Week:

Month:

AFFIRMATION:
I show confidence and positivity wherever I go.

JOURNAL PROMPT:
How do I show confidence in my everyday life?

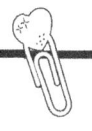

DRAW A PICTURE OF YOURSELF BEING CONFIDENT AND COLOR IT!

Weekly Affirmations

Week:

Month:

AFFIRMATION:
I am a reflection of my ancestors' strength and wisdom.

JOURNAL PROMPT:
What is a positive lesson I've learned from someone in my family or culture?

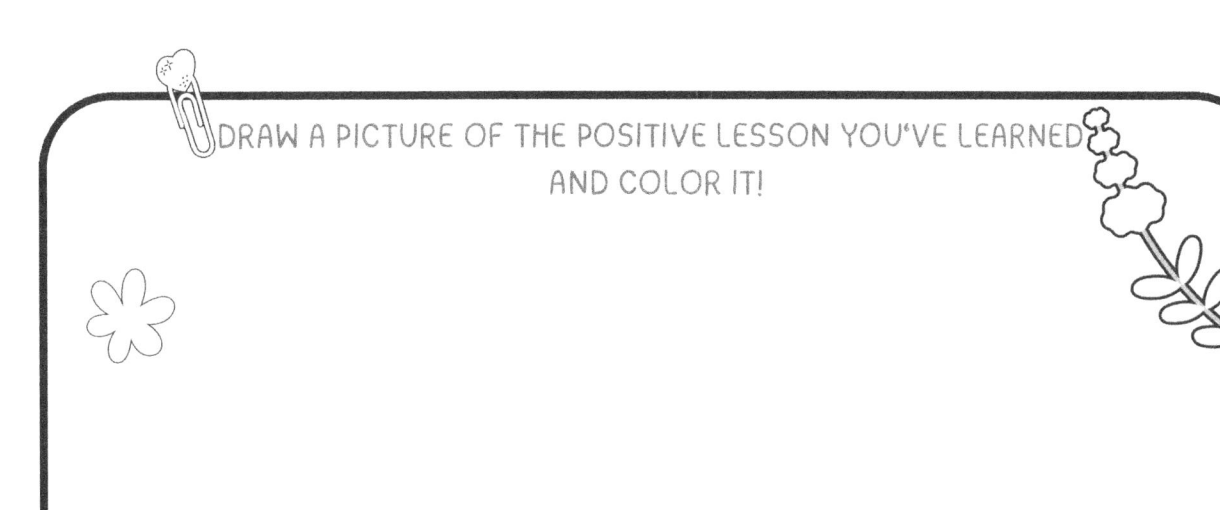

DRAW A PICTURE OF THE POSITIVE LESSON YOU'VE LEARNED AND COLOR IT!

Weekly

Week:

Month:

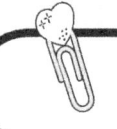

AFFIRMATION:
I am proud of the young Black girl I am becoming.

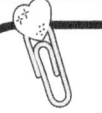

JOURNAL PROMPT:
Name some qualities that you are proud of having.
Why are these qualities important to my future?

June Affirmations

- I can and I will....
- I love myself.
- I am preparing for greatness.
- My dreams are in my reach.
- I am confident in my abilities.

I am BRAVE

good things are coming

Weekly Affirmations

Week:

Month:

AFFIRMATION:
I deserve my voice to be heard.

JOURNAL PROMPT:
Think about a time I felt proud to speak my truth. What did I learn?

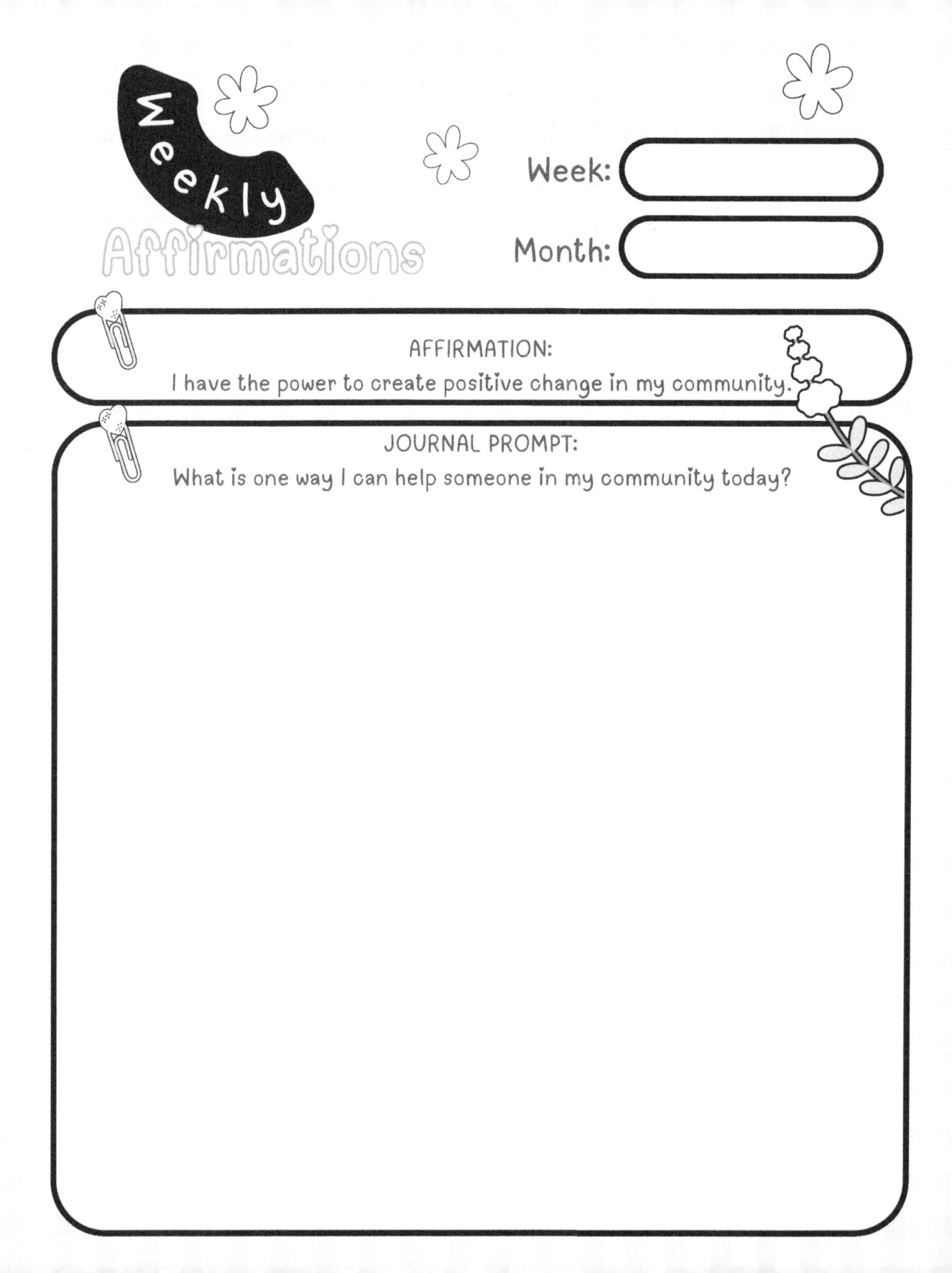

Weekly Affirmations

Week:

Month:

AFFIRMATION:
I have the power to create positive change in my community.

JOURNAL PROMPT:
What is one way I can help someone in my community today?

DRAW A PICTURE OF YOU HELPING SOMEONE AND COLOR IT!

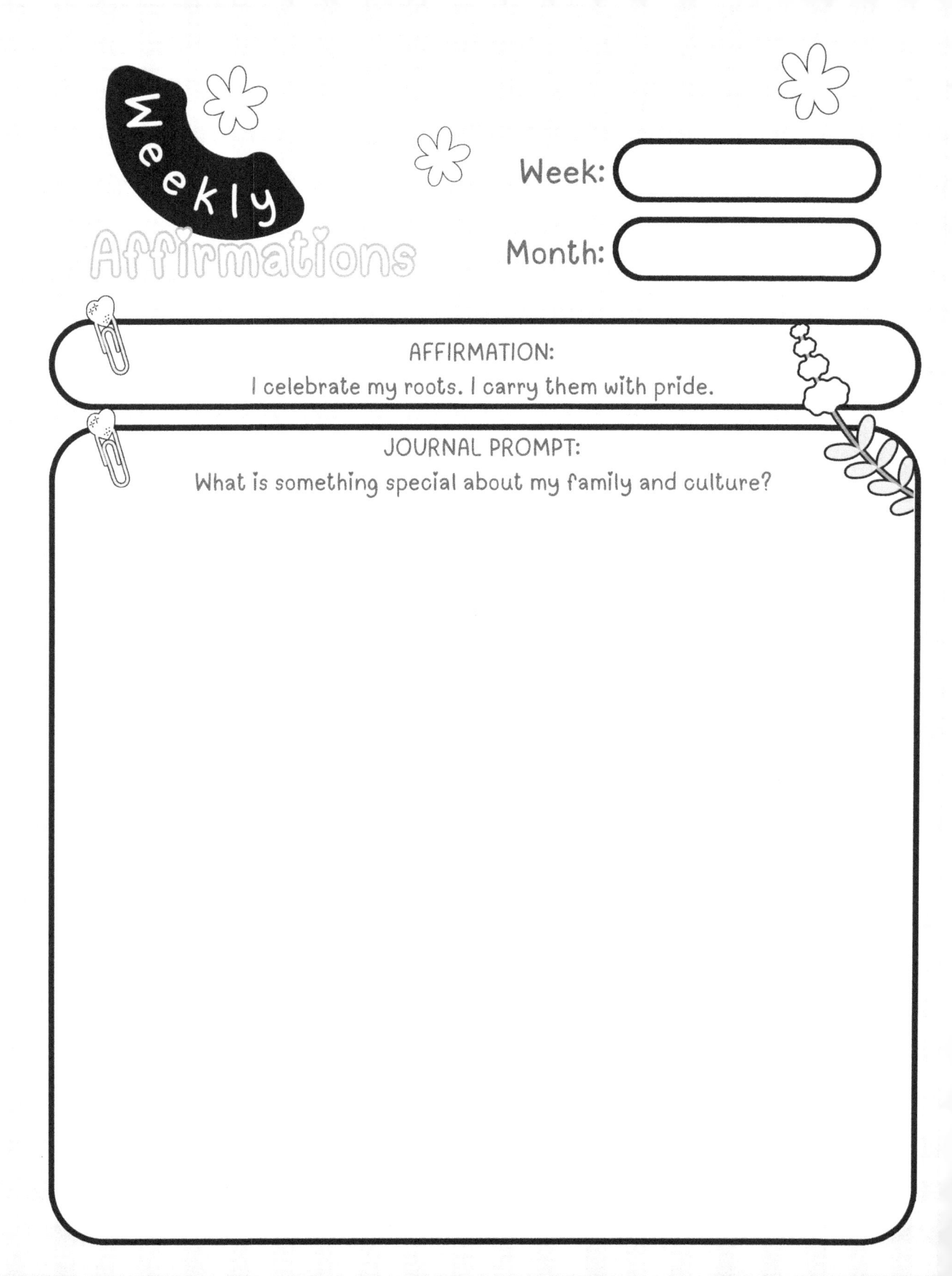

Weekly Affirmations

Week:

Month:

AFFIRMATION:
I celebrate my roots. I carry them with pride.

JOURNAL PROMPT:
What is something special about my family and culture?

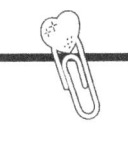

DRAW A PICTURE OF IT AND COLOR IT!

Weekly Affirmations

Week:

Month:

AFFIRMATION:
I love every part of me even the parts I'm still learning to love.

JOURNAL PROMPT:
What is one thing about me I'm learning to feel more confident about?

DRAW A PICTURE OF IT AND COLOR IT!

July Affirmations

I make my ancestors proud.

I am a game changer.

I am created perfectly in God's image.

I deserve to be protected and respected.

I will grow up to be a great person.

BEING YOU IS YOUR *power*

I am stronger ~than~ yesterday

Weekly

Week:

Month:

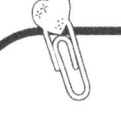

AFFIRMATION:
I focus on my blessings and good things.

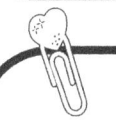

JOURNAL PROMPT:
What is something that made me smile this week?
Why was it special?

Weekly Affirmations

Week:

Month:

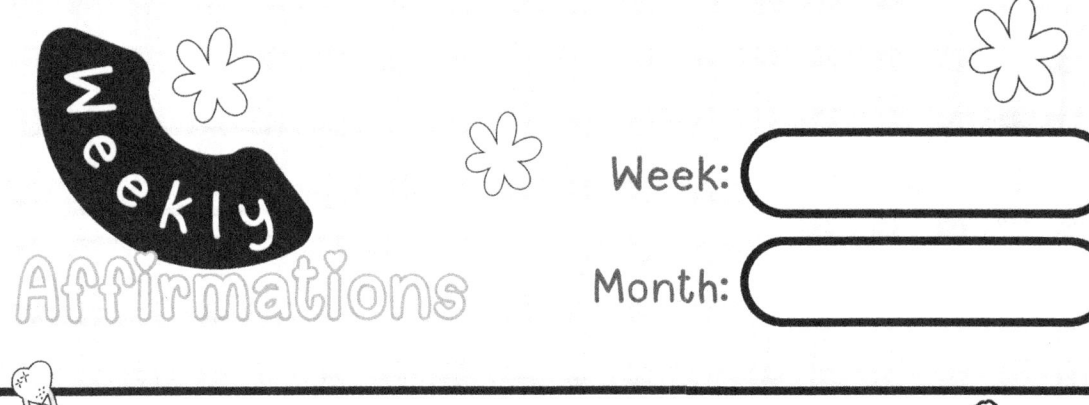

AFFIRMATION:
I am strong, beautiful, and capable.

JOURNAL PROMPT:
Think about a time when I overcame a challenge.
How did that experience make me feel stronger?

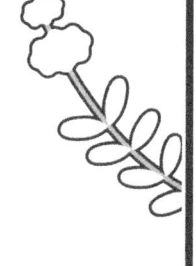

DRAW A PICTURE OF YOURSELF OVERCOMING THE CHALLENGE AND COLOR IT!

Weekly Affirmations

Week:

Month:

AFFIRMATION:
My Black culture is a beautiful gift. I am proud to be a part of it.

JOURNAL PROMPT:
How does being a Black girl make me unique and special?

DRAW A PICTURE OF YOUR UNIQUENESS AND COLOR IT!

Weekly Affirmations

Week:

Month:

AFFIRMATION:
I am thankful for my family and their love for me!

JOURNAL PROMPT:
What does family mean to me?

August Affirmations

It's the curls for me!

My afro is enough.

My dreams can become my reality.

I can make it out of my circumstances.

My skin tone, features, and hair texture are unique and beautiful.

INHALE EXHALE repeat

HIP HOP

I accept myself as I am

Weekly Affirmations

Week:

Month:

AFFIRMATION:
I create my path. I walk it with confidence.

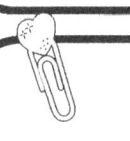

JOURNAL PROMPT:
What is a big goal I want to achieve this year?

DRAW A PICTURE OF YOURSELF ACHIEVING YOUR GOAL AND COLOR IT!

Weekly Affirmations

Week:

Month:

AFFIRMATION:
I deserve success and joy.

JOURNAL PROMPT:
What do I want to be when I grow up and why?

DRAW A PICTURE OF YOU WORKING IN YOUR FUTURE CAREER AND COLOR IT!

Weekly Affirmations

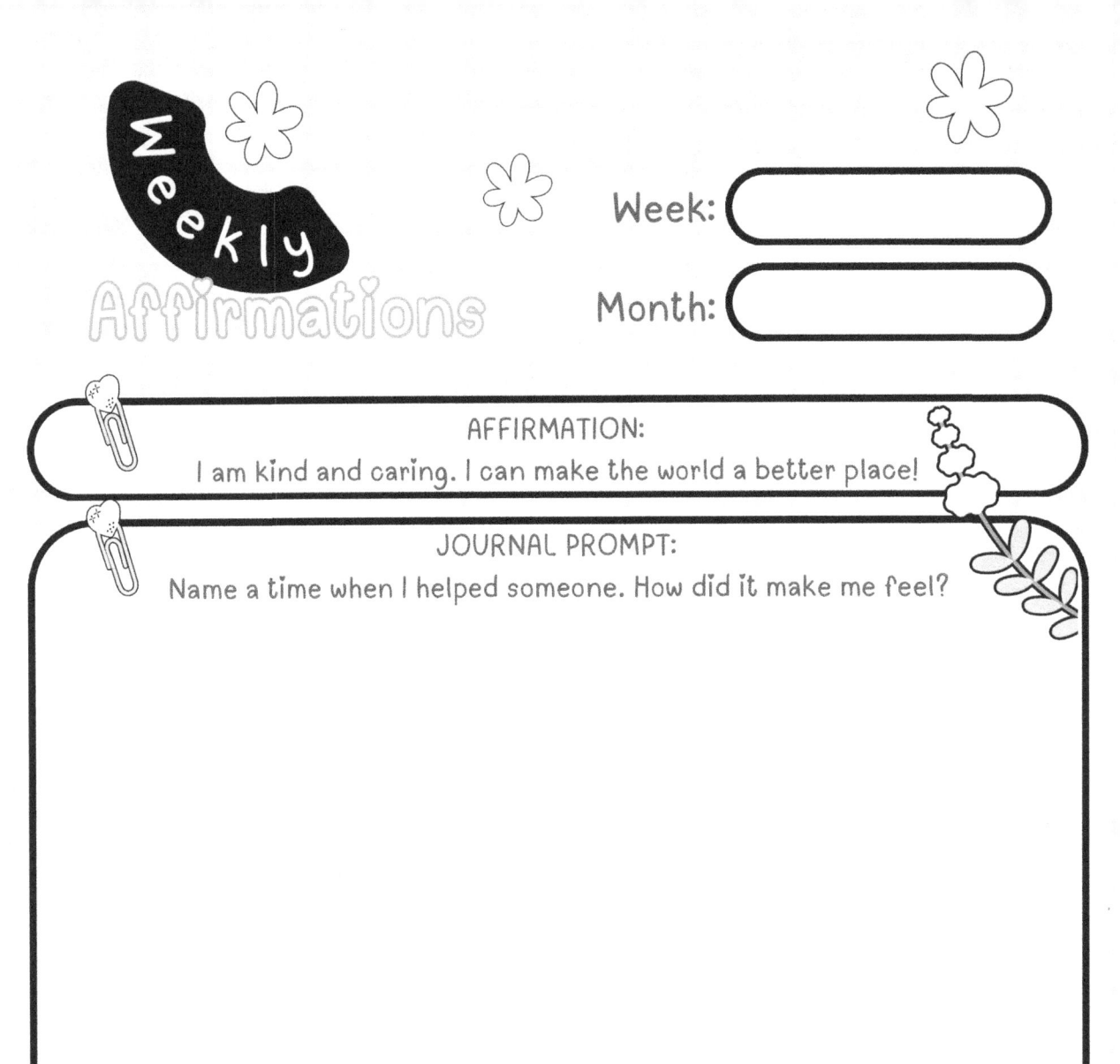

Week:

Month:

AFFIRMATION:
I am kind and caring. I can make the world a better place!

JOURNAL PROMPT:
Name a time when I helped someone. How did it make me feel?

DRAW A PICTURE OF YOU HELPING SOMEONE AND COLOR IT!

Weekly Affirmations

Week:

Month:

AFFIRMATION:
I celebrate my growth.

JOURNAL PROMPT:
What are some ways I want to grow this year?

September Affirmations

- I am preparing for greatness.
- I wear my crown with pride.
- I respect and honor my family.
- I respect and honor myself.
- I deserve respect in all spaces.

I am proud of myself!

I make myself a priority

Weekly Affirmations

Week:

Month:

AFFIRMATION:
I am becoming the best version of myself.

JOURNAL PROMPT:
What are some things I am working on to become a better me?

Weekly Affirmations

Week:

Month:

AFFIRMATION:
I am unique. I stand out proudly!

JOURNAL PROMPT:
What makes me stand out from others?

DRAW A PICTURE OF WHY YOU STAND OUT AND COLOR IT!

Weekly Affirmations

Week:

Month:

AFFIRMATION:
I am worthy of love and respect.

JOURNAL PROMPT:
How do I show myself love every day?

DRAW A PICTURE OF YOU SHOWING YOURSELF LOVE AND COLOR IT!

Weekly Affirmations

Week:

Month:

AFFIRMATION:
Others' unkind words do not change how I feel about me.
I am awesome and I know it!

JOURNAL PROMPT:
Think about a time someone said something unkind about me.
I know it's not true because…

October Affirmations

I believe in me.

I can make it through hard days.

I am thankful!

I am brave!

I will fight for what is right.

I am CAPABLE

I deserve good things

Weekly Affirmations

Week:

Month:

AFFIRMATION:
I am proud of how far I've come.

JOURNAL PROMPT:
Think about how far you've grown over the years.
What are you most proud of?

Weekly Affirmations

Week:

Month:

AFFIRMATION:
I am a light in this world.

JOURNAL PROMPT:
What are some ways I show my confidence?

Weekly Affirmations

Week:

Month:

AFFIRMATION:
I am not perfect and it's okay!

JOURNAL PROMPT:
What is something I have learned to love about myself?

Weekly Affirmations

Week:

Month:

AFFIRMATION:
I am becoming the best version of myself.

JOURNAL PROMPT:
What is one lesson I have learned that made me a better person?

November Affirmations

My style is how I express myself.

I got this!

I believe great things will happen.

My future is bright.

I embrace my growth.

have a grateful heart

TODAY -I am- THANKFUL

Weekly Affirmations

Week:

Month:

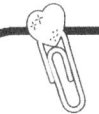

AFFIRMATION:
I am a leader! It is okay not to follow the crowd.

JOURNAL PROMPT:
Think about a time I made my own choice instead of following others. How did it feel to be a leader?

Weekly Affirmations

Week:

Month:

AFFIRMATION:
My natural hair is my crown. I gladly wear it on my head with pride!

JOURNAL PROMPT:
What are some favorite ways I style my natural curls that make me feel beautiful?

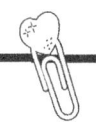

DRAW A PICTURE OF YOUR FAVORITE HAIRSTYLES AND COLOR IT!

Weekly Affirmations

Week:

Month:

AFFIRMATION:
I can see a brighter future beyond where I am right now.

JOURNAL PROMPT:
Think about my future. What is something I am excited about that I don't have in my life now?

DRAW A PICTURE OF WHAT YOU SEE IN YOUR FUTURE AND COLOR IT!

Weekly Affirmations

Week:

Month:

AFFIRMATION:

I treat my parents (or my _____) with respect because *(grandparents, aunt/uncle, sister/brother, guardian, etc.)* they are taking care of me.

JOURNAL PROMPT:

Name some things that my parents (or my _____) do to take *(grandparents, aunt/uncle, sister/brother, guardian, etc.)* good care of me.

December Affirmations

I am a piece of art.

I am a good person.

I show others respect and kindness.

I am supported and accepted.

I am worthy and valuable!

I matter!

I am proud of myself!

Weekly Affirmations

Week:

Month:

AFFIRMATION:
My beautiful skin color tells a story. It deserves to be celebrated!

JOURNAL PROMPT:
How do I celebrate my skin tone?
What are some colors I like to wear that make my skin tone sparkle?

Weekly Affirmations

Week:

Month:

AFFIRMATION:
I love my family. I honor and respect them.

JOURNAL PROMPT:
Write a letter to a family member who has inspired or supported me.
Why am I thankful for them?
(Let them read how much they mean to you).

Weekly Affirmations

Week:

Month:

AFFIRMATION:
I love my friends. I honor and respect them.

JOURNAL PROMPT:
Write a letter to a friend. Why do I value our friendship?
(Let them read how much they mean to you).

Weekly Affirmations

Week:

Month:

AFFIRMATION:
I close this year thankful for all the blessings, love, and good things that surround me.

JOURNAL PROMPT:
Think about the many positive things that happened this year. Name some things for which I am thankful.

Write your own Affirmations!

YOUR GOALS are important

I Deserve to be Happy

Made in the USA
Las Vegas, NV
05 March 2025

19081259R00057